Cannabis recipes and extracts and how to use them

THE NEVERENDING STORY OF CANNABIS EXTRACTS - The types of concentrates and their method of extraction -

Table of Contents

THE PROCESS OF EXTRACTION 10

Oxidation – the degradation of THC into CBN 13

Decarboxylation – the conversion of THC-A into THC 14

EXTRACTS 16

Kief 16

Hashish 19

Butane Hash Oil 21

The Rosin Tech 23

Rick Simpson oil – alcohol extraction 24

Tincture 26

Olive oil extraction 27

Cannabutter 28

Cannamilk 29

Cookies 30

Cannabis extracts constitute an entire universe, once you've stepped inside you might get lost in the multitude of extraction products that can be consumed in multiple ways, some of which are at this very moment being imagined. In fact, this is what keeps an entire industry going and growing – the imagination and perseverance of the passionate souls. Those who are developing more and more efficient techniques, experimenting, playing, failing but keeping on and in the end developing specific methods for their specific needs. The medical marijuana industry draws its roots as well as its amazing continual improvement and expansion to the few of us that prepare our medicines at home, the way we like it and share the knowledge with the rest of the family. Sharing and caring is what we owe to this plant in first place.

So, if you tend to be caring and receptive towards cannabis, for sure you would be mesmerized by its extracted forms as each has its unique manifestation in your mind and body. Whether you inhale or ingest, the route it takes through your body, how long it takes to be infused into your cells and take effect as well as its duration, the potency of the different formulas, the particular interplay of cannabinoids in various strains. The possibility to "design" the perfect one for you is there, but be careful as your perfect one will never be the same; you can get absorbed into this world, into this quest.

But this is not an unprecedented fame, as cannabis has been traditionally used by ancient cultures around the globe and almost all modern methods are very similar to the ones our ancestors were practicing for physical and spiritual healing, for calming the body and the mind.

Smoking the plant upon a hill, sharing the pipe with the other tribe members, celebrating the blissful moment of universal connection, was just one of the many rituals as well as routines that involved marijuana. It was praised for its psycho-active effects that alter the mind and send you through a reflective, meditative journey with a transformative potential, illuminating and curing your being.

As such, people used to put the marijuana flowers in a piece of fabric, weaved from some natural fiber and hang it over the fire. The heat would make the resin melt and slowly begin to leak – a bowl was placed underneath to collect the oil; the rest was scraped from the fabric.

This is the primitive equivalent of the currently trending Rosin tech which makes use of a heat press (hair straightened, iron, t-shirt press) instead of the old wood fire in the open air and parchment or cooking paper that can be much easily scraped than the rough texture of hemp fiber. So of course, in terms of efficiency, a lot more material was wasting away in the wind and it was way more time consuming to produce resin by the means of a tribal man.

But back then, people had all the time in the world for whatever gave them peace and spending a night under the stars preparing your stuff was part of the whole ritual. Not to mention that in those immemorial times, all plants and virtually all there was, was free for men to consume as they liked, no self-established authority to censor their appetite, their curiosity, their self-discovery journey, their peace of mind.

It wasn't until a few centuries ago that the prohibition succeeded to eliminate cannabis from people's consciences, to alienate their minds so profoundly as not only to forget but to deny such an important part of their collective individuality. Before that, from South America to Europe, men were mental traveling through the Milky Way – they were preparing marijuana milk extracts as routine.

The habit of giving a few sips of a milk extract to agitated restless children, in the evenings before going to sleep, is something that a modern citizen would denounce to child support institutions. But at the same time, I've been hearing this from my elders and stumbling upon it in the most diverse places, under diverse cultural climates – people were naturally doing it and we'd now call them crazy for it. They must have put their trust in nature and in themselves much more than we now do, they must have been freer in their minds and in their lives, they must have known something.

So why are extracts booming on the medical marijuana market and on the streets?

Recent years have meant a huge leap forward for the medial use of marijuana, projected in the legal reforms that allow its use, production and selling, although of course restricted to certain states. But this move has pushed forward research and has set in motion a mechanism that will turn people's attention towards the healing properties of this magical herb, ultimately changing mentalities and unchaining this natural organism.

Medically, marijuana has been used to treat and ease such a huge variety of conditions from inducing appetite and over-all relief for cancer patients, HIV, for reducing muscle spasms and helping ones that suffer from Parkinson, decreasing pain and aiding those with chronic headaches, affecting sclerosis, arthritis, depression. And these are just a few.

As its cannabinoids constituents have perfectly mirroring receptors in our body, that once activated can generate a complete systemic refresh of the organism, one can only imagine that cannabis could be a universal panacea.

For medical purposes, extracts are recommended because of their potency – while buds may contain between 10 to 25% THC, the extract compounds exhibit 50 to 80%. But there is also another level of purity in extracts, as in the process of obtaining them you also get rid of a lot of residues and retain only the active substances.

Of course, as any enthusiast knows, that dabbing some resin or placing some tincture on your gums is going to take your high to a whole other dimension – the effect is much more profound and psychedelic. It lasts a lot longer and it works differently, it smoothly insinuates inside your body and your mind and the overall impression is that consuming cannabis in this manner seems to be more natural.

And without the extracts we couldn't indulge ourselves in the tastiest cookies, prepared with simple canna butter or canna coconut butter, lollipops, crackers, energy balls and the list can endlessly go on. When in a state where marijuana consumption is legal, you feel like walking through the wonderland, as every family has its own special recipe to consume cannabis.

This comprehensive guide will introduce you to the different types of cannabis extracts along with their particular extracting methods. You will learn the subtle differences between end-products, their benefits and their special way of use. Thus, you will be able to choose the one that fits your needs and desires.

But most of all, it will be a journey that will reveal the incredible medicinal value of cannabis constituents and the way each interacts with your body and mind, as extracts are meant to concentrate one (THC), some or all of these compounds.

Engaging in preparing your own medicine is a most precious activity that will transform the simple act of consuming into a complete ritual. You would be literally impregnating the extract with your own energy and healing intention – though this is not something that you can scientifically calculate or prove, for sure its end effect is utterly priceless.

THE PROCESS OF EXTRACTION

Most of us will throw themselves head-down in this quest of obtaining the most potent concentrate, but any option you'd choose, you'll learn soon enough that this a complex procedure. Extracting is the art of processing the plant while maintaining the subtle equilibrium between concentration, purity and as much of the initial constituency as possible. It is almost like an alchemical undertakes to come up with the most exquisite cannabis gold.

And the first to be established are your premises: what do you need the extract for? Do you want it to be high in THC, CBD, do you want to get rid of the extra cannabinoids and terpenes. Do you want to eat it or dab it?

Most practitioners focus their attention on THC, because as everybody knows, this the particular substance provoking the high. But there has been a lot of research done in this area and though little is yet known about the others cannabinoids, one important statement has been made. Apparently, the effect that cannabis has is due to the interaction of all substances and not just one.

Terpenes for example, are fragrance oils reclaimed to endorse the weed with its unique flavor, they were thought to bring to the play only the olfactory effect, but recent studies have proved differently – they also contribute to the specific characteristic of the high. Just a couple of examples: Limonene is responsible for the citrus smell and works as an antidepressant, elevating your mood and aiding the gastric reflux, while Pinene with its sharp, fresh pine flavor is anti-inflammatory, bronchodilator and works on your alertness and memory. These are just two from a wild variety – to get an idea just imagine the multitude of flavors that you've sensed in the different types of weed and understand that each is connected with a particular influence.

I'll try to better explain the interplay of chemical compounds in cannabis, by telling you about the most powerful extract that you can find on the market. Be sure you're seated, as this will blow your mind and you'd probably pass out.

Crystalline THC-A hash (THC-A is the precursor of THC, read on and you will learn more about its conversion when heated) has a 99.9 % THC concentration so it's virtually the strongest possible form your buds can take. Its appearance is as surprising – it's like a conglomerate of crystals, looking almost too much like the synthetic crystal-meth instead of your natural pot. Having the maximum THC purity, this hash has no other cannabinoids or terpenes, is odorless and tasteless. When you buy it from a medical marijuana shop you will be offered some extra oils containing either CBD or different terpenes, in which to dip the little piece of Crystalline before dabbing it.

The most interesting part comes when you read people's reviews about its high. And it is nothing like you imagined – apparently, in terms of potency it is comparable to the common butane hash oil, but this before adding the extra oils. Afterwards, the story changes and the effect uplifts to what it should be expected. So why is its effect amplified when CBD and terpenes are added? Is it our mind that recognizes the well-known taste and smell and only then triggers the high in the body, or is it because the high is to be expected when all the cannabinoids and the terpenes work together?

The user's testimonies point out also that the type of high produced by this magical hash is a more balanced one, it comes with a lot more clarity. It transports you to a trance dimension indeed, but one that leaves up to its name – a crystal clear state of mind.

This also makes you think about the importance of purity to the over-all effect. The Crystalline hash definitely has no degraded cannabinoids (read further about the degradation of THC) and its means of preparation involve no chemical solvents, which in its turn produces the purest high.

The different methods of extraction and the chemical solvents used to perform them, are the coordinates that make out for the appearance of the oils, some are honey-yellow, others dark-brown, some are glassy and transfused, others fluid and opaque. Surprisingly the natural form of THC is the crystallized one.

Before engaging in any extraction method, you should understand the natural processes that the cannabis constituents undergo. There's little being said about this phenomenon, but without knowing the chemical interaction and reaction to exterior stimuli, you might end up with a useless extract.

Oxidation – the degradation of THC into CBN

Primarily, all plant extracts and concentrates have the purpose of preserving the medicinal active compounds, that otherwise start to degrade, depending on the method of storage but regardless of that. It is simply the effect of time on the dried plant.

For cannabis, the process of degradation consists in the oxidation of the THC cannabinoids in a compound called CBN, which also stands for the decrease in the weed's potency in time. But CBN contributes as well to the over-all psychotropic effect of cannabis adding a somewhat dizzy sensation resembling that produced by alcohol, diverting and deterring the clarity of mind that is otherwise provided by a purer concentrate.

The conversion into CBN is accelerated when cannabis is exposed to heat, thus through all methods of extraction and of course the moment you light up your bud to smoke it. But heat is absolutely necessary in order to enjoy the effects of THC (as you'll learn further on) so the problem that remains to be solved is the concentration of CBN in the compound you are using. And extraction, though producing it throughout the process, at the end, puts this natural phenomenon on a standstill (the passing of time will have little or no effect on shatter, hash or oil, until you light it up of course).

Decarboxylation – the conversion of THC-A into THC

This chemical progression is the key to your high. Without it, the psychoactive cannabinoids in your weed would be null. You've probably didn't even hear about it and if you tend to smoke, vaporize or dab your buds, then it's not even necessary to know it. But if you're planning on preparing tincture or cookies, then you better read it carefully otherwise your extract will come with a not so pleasant surprise. It actually explains why drinking juice out of raw weed will have no effect whatsoever.

THCA (tetrahydrocannabinolic acid) is the non-active precursor of THC. It is this compound that is contained in the cannabis plant, fresh, dried or processed without heat. And it is precisely heat that sparks the conversion of THCA into the psychoactive THC. During this chemical reaction, the cannabinoids lose one carbon atom which makes its structure symmetric to that of our own receptors.

As with oxidation, this transformation can also happen naturally but it can take virtually years.

Therefore, you must artificially activate the THC by applying heat. And this can vary depending on the product you're using. If you want to use kief, you only need to put it in something hot like coffee or tea and it almost instantly converts, for hash it takes a bit longer but still if you add it to your food before cooking it, it will be ready along with your dish. But plant matter takes even longer so it becomes mandatory to bake it in an oven before actually extracting it.

Here's how you do it:

Put the trim and buds on a Pyrex glass plate (also known as Yenna glass), on a pizza stone, in the oven at 105° C for about 45 minutes.

There is a lot controversy around this procedure, especially regarding the temperature, as different compounds in the cannabis plant have different boiling points. And because of this it requires maximum of attention because otherwise your weed will start gradually losing potency, first the terpenes and flavonoids and afterwards the cannabinoids.

The temperature I've suggested allows you to "play safe". Some recommend 115° C for 30 minutes, but considering that most home ovens have uncontrollable fluctuations I think it's best not to risk. Moreover, if you want to keep as much terpenes and flavonoids after decarboxylation than it's better to perform it at even lower temperatures, adjusting the time accordingly (the lower the temp – the longer the duration)

Decarboxylation is not necessary when you're extracting cannabis in oil or milk as the boiling temperatures and duration of these operations are enough to complete the transition to an active end product.

EXTRACTS

There are two big categories of extracts – those that you dab or vape and those that you ingest or use sublingual. The immense variety of end-products doesn't reflect in a similar variety of high effects, though. Because it is mainly due to the means of production and most of all, the substances used as solvents.

I recommend the cleaner and most non-invasive solvents and the simplest, as closest to natural methods. The differences between extracts are so subtle that there is really no need to get into complicated techniques.

We've come a long way creatively and scientifically that it became almost pointless to use potentially dangerous substances as butane gas to obtain the same hash that you can otherwise get it by simply heating and pressing your buds as in the Rosin technique.

For the sake of knowledge though and as a starting point to any new practices, I will mention all main methods.

Kief

What we call kief are in fact the marijuana's plant trachoma glands. These resin glands that can be found all over the plant but are massively grouped around buds and close-by leaves; also, to be found on male plants, though in a considerably smaller quantity. They are the laboratories where the cannabinoids, terpenes and flavonoids are produced and stored. So kief is exactly what you're looking for in the cannabis plant.

The trachoma's look like minuscule hairs covering the plant. They change their color with the growth of the plant so when it is mature, the glands will be dark-yellow to brown.

Anyone using a three piece grinder knows what kief is. Or if you don't, then shame on you. These grinders have a special compartment where kief is deposited – a sift is used to keep the grinded bud and let the kief drop bellow and be collected afterwards. *When the moment comes to open up that little vault, it's absolutely mesmerizing because it will have mixed all the different tastes and aromas of the weeds that you've used during this period into one potent and rich concentrate.*

If you want to produce larger quantities, you will have to improvise a sifting box. The trachoma is extremely small and sticky so it's not easy to separate them from the rest of the plant material. That's why it would be helpful to make an installation with a few sifting screens placed one on top of the other, the densest one at the bottom. And shake.

A good trick is to place one or a few coins on the screen, in the box. While shaking it, the coins will scratch the screen and this will ease the process.

The purest form of kief obtained after severe sifting is called **dry sieve** or dry sift.

Kief can be spread on the buds that you smoke to potentiate your stash or it can even be dissolved into your morning coffee cup or evening tea.

It can also be used for cooking and it doesn't need decarboxylation, as its dusty structure permits it to undergo this process easily at lower temperatures.

The original and most simple way of making hash is in fact by applying heat and pressure to kief – this ruptures the resin glands structure and makes them stick together while changing their color to darker brown.

Here's a simple method to do it at home, using an iron:

Put the kief on a parchment paper and fold it in two. Cover the parchment with another protective layer like a piece of cloth or a towel. Set the iron at its lowest temperature and press for 3-4 seconds, and then lift it. Repeat this action for about 20 times, checking and flipping your parchment from one side to the other.

Hashish

The myth says that the first men to make hash were the growers harvesting their crops. While handling the plants, the resin got stuck to their hands and rubbing each hand left them with small bits of sticky brown matter that could be afterwards recomposed into small balls of hash.

Hash is the cleanest cannabis extract as its production doesn't imply the use of any chemical solvents and the techniques have been developed and perfected during centuries, but all mainly draw from the same principle stated above: gluing together the plants resin glands.

The advantage of making hash is that you can dramatically reduce the plant material that is otherwise wasted. From the whole cannabis plant, we usually only consume the buds and rarely the trim, but trachoma is to be found all over, on the stalk as well as on all its leaves. And it can all be processed into hash.

One common method to make hash is with ice cubes. I'll explain the way it works by using a blender, which will be practical for small quantities and it will also give you an idea to improvise for larger amounts.

Cold water will help the plant to loosen the glands. They are heavier than water so they will drop to the bottom; while the plant itself is lighter therefore it will float at the top.

Just place the cannabis in a blender along with ice cubes and water. Blend them and stir the contents into a jar. Let it settle for about half an hour, afterwards you'll observe that the smallest plant parts have lifted to the top, while the resin remained on the bottom. Drain approximately two thirds of the water, being careful not to disturb or drain the resin, then add some more freezing water and let it rest again.

After some time, when the resin has settled again, repeat the operation. The third time strain the contents of the jar through a coffee filter, pressing it well to eliminate any excess water and you've got your own chunk of hash.

For a completely scrupulous procedure – cold wash the plant material for a second, maybe even third time, to be sure that all resin has been removed and transformed in hash.

This technique employs primeval means (except the use of the blender which is anyway optional) but it works out perfectly. A more sophisticated alternative that is evidently more precise but as well more complicated, operates with liquid nitrogen. Fundamentally it follows the same formula, but it detaches the trachoma more efficiently and almost instantly – when processing cannabis into **nitrohash** you can be sure that you've optimally extracted all the goodies.

Butane Hash Oil

This most dangerous and as well the most widely used method to obtain hash oil, the honey oil that we all know so well. It is the most efficient in terms of the concentration – the butane hash oil can have up to 80-90 % THC and it can be rendered to process massive amounts of weed in a relatively short time.

But also, it's the one technique responsible for too many accidents, injuries, blown-up houses and even deaths.

And still, the reason I'm not recommending it is not the high jeopardy risk. As long as you're not exposing anyone else to the perils of this procedure, you are free to do whatever you please with your own life.

But the butane gas has its own doze of impurities that cannot be eliminated or controlled. It does evaporate completely but the residues pre-contained by it, remain in your extract and they may be potentially more dangerous on the long term than the momentary leak of gas.

As it is the most common extraction option around, I will expand it for those of you who are curious, but strongly advise the courageous ones to better research before trying this.

First of all, be sure not purchase lowers grade butane because it most probably has more irremovable residues. You will need 8 oz. butane for 30 grams weed.

This process should be performed outside as butane gas is heavier than air so even in a well ventilated chamber, if it leaks the gas will float in lower area and explode at the slightest spark.

You will also need a stainless steel tube that you will fill with the pot to be extracted. It's important that you improvise some sort of stander for it. Pack the weed inside. For perfectly clean yellow honey oil it's better to use whole buds. They should be fitted inside the tube so as to have as less air pockets as you can, none is the ideal; but at the same time, you shouldn't press it, the butane has to flow freely, otherwise it creates pressure.

In the meantime, prepare a Pyrex dish where your extract will leak and place it under the tube. Also put a pan with water on the fire, big enough to contain the Pyrex dish.

Start injecting butane in 30 seconds cycles interrupted by 15-20 seconds breaks, until you empty the gas tank. The extracted compound along with the liquid butane will discharge into you Pyrex dish. Just wait till it stops dripping. Then place the dish in the water pan.

! Be careful – the water shouldn't be boiling but just hot. The freezing butane extraction may produce a devastating reaction if in contact with boiling water!

Shortly afterwards, your solution will start bubbling, it's the butane getting evaporated – wait and enjoy the show. When there are very few to no bubbles at all left, the dish should be put on a heating pad to eliminate all the rest of the butane. It's extremely important to be sure that the whole process is successfully finished and it should be after about an hour.

What will remain on the dish is exclusively the honey oil that, if everything is performed as instructed, should be a beautiful glassy shatter, that you'd have to scrape off. Of course, it can also be lower grade hash oil, darker and more opaque or even more sticky or fluid, but this all depends on the quality of used products as well as your over-all performance.

The Rosin Tech

This resin processing technique has recently made a huge hype around the world because it's extremely easy to perform and what you obtain is a crystal perfect shatter. Most probably it will soon replace the more complicated and aggressive methods, as the butane gas one.

The one who discovered it is a passionate soul like you and me, who then shared it with everybody else. And the funniest thing is that he stumbled upon it by mistake while trying to turn a second grade hash into some better dabbing material.

All you need is a hair straightened, a piece of parchment and some good buds. Applying pressure and heat to the buds will crush the trachoma and make the resin leak out of the bud. It's the same procedure that you use to make hash out of kief. Afterwards, just scrape the resin off the parchment.

For larger quantities you can use a t-shirt press with the same success.

Rick Simpson oil – alcohol extraction

So called after the man who perfected this ancient method and promoted it. As the above butane oil, this extraction method is also widely used and is responsible for most of the edible hash oil to be found on and off the market.

As opposed to the butane, the alcohol extraction is less damaging to the complex constituency of the cannabis plant. And most importantly, it can be ingested.

What you will get is dark color dense but slightly fluid oil.

For this you will need a high grade alcohol (90% or higher).

Put the weed in a bucket or a large bowl and pour the alcohol. Crush the weed with a wooden spoon, stick or anything similar, be sure that it is well covered with solvent. Continue to crush and stir the plant material in the alcohol – as you do this the extraction takes place.

After about 3-5 minutes, strain the mix in another container, take the plant material back and repeat the process with a new solvent. After stirring for another 3-5 minutes, strain it over the old one. To be sure that you've taken everything you can from your weed, you can extract it for a third time, but most surely you got about 80 % the first time you did it. Using a coffee filter, you can sift the whole quantity again to get rid of any impurity.

You now have two options: letting the alcohol evaporate naturally, which will take a long time and you'll need to go through the decarboxylation process if you want to ingest the oil as it; or boil the mix to help the alcohol evaporate much faster.

If you choose boiling, you should be aware not to go over 105° C and constantly check it. When the level of liquid has lowered, put a few drops of water inside – it will help the solvent to be eliminated completely along with residues. When there's about 1 inch of solvent left, take the pot and easily swing it on the fire, until there's nothing left but the hash oil. You're not done just yet – even if you can't spot it, there is still the water left inside your compound and you have to eliminate it, but this time in a less aggressive heater, a coffee device or a dehydrator. Examining the liquid, you will notice some bubbling activity at the surface and only when this stops, you hash oil is ready to be stored.

Tincture

Making tinctures is one old traditional method to retain the medicinal properties of herbs. The active compounds are extracted in alcohol and the way to use cannabis tincture is to put a few drops under your tongue.

It's for sure a must try because the effect is very pleasant – you will start feeling high in about 15-20 minutes, as opposed to other edibles that go through your stomach and take a couple of hours to be digested and infused in all your cells. But the tincture's effect lasts as long as other concentrates so after a few hours you will still be able to feel high.

You will need higher grade alcohol (90% or higher), as in Rick Simpson method, but this time you won't let it evaporate, but instead let the plant be macerated into the solvent for a longer period of time. You will have to decarb your weed first, because there will no exposure to heat through this technique.

For about 1 gram of weed use 35 ml alcohol – so do your math.

The weed should be left to soak in alcohol, in a glass jar, for 5-10 days. By experimenting you will discover by yourself the perfect cycle of time. Do not keep the container in direct sunlight. Shake the jar once a day to make the mix homogenous. At the end of the period, strain the contents of the jar through a coffee filter and store it in a dark glass medicine bottle. Be sure to have an eye-dropper attached to your bottle as it will only take a few drops to make you reasonably high.

Olive oil extraction

Olive oil is very efficient for extracting active compounds from a lot of medicinal plants. And it works great with weed. Moreover, the greasy substances (milk and butter as well) are excellent for retaining most of the active cannabinoids, terpenes and flavonoids.

Only when extracting in oil, milk or butter you can use raw, not dried weed. Some might say this way you won't benefit the maximum potency that your batch is able to produce. But I say that this is exactly the contrary, because raw weed has much fewer degraded compounds, the cannabinoids just haven't had the time to convert and the terpenes and flavonoids are also still there as they were when the plant was still in the ground.

For about 100 grams of weed you can use about one liter of olive oil.

Put the oil and the plant material in a pot. Crush or blend the buds to fit in and sit covered in oil. And then cook it at 105° for about two hours. For this you should use two pots, one with sun flower cooking oil and the other containing your mix, above or in the first.
When the cooking is done, let it wait till it cools down and then put it in a blender and smash it well. After it will rest, the plant material will lower to the bottom and the oil will be easily drained and added to your favorite dishes.

Also, the same process can be performed with coconut oil, if you prefer it.

Cannabutter

Cannabutter is great because it leaves you with a lot of possibilities, from cooking it into a cake, to adding it to popcorn or simply spreading it on a slice of toast.

For this you will have to grind you cannabis buds. And the quantities are 500 grams butter for about 15 grams of weed. Place the butter in a pan and only when it's melted, pour the weed, stirring with a wood spoon – careful not to stick either to the bottom or the pan's walls or your butter will taste as if burned. Let it cook at minimum temperature for about 3 hours. When it's done and it has cooled enough you can use a French press to strain it. Then place it in another container and put it in the fridge.

Cannamilk

This Milky Way extract is one special treat that will carry you across the galaxy. It's one very simple method to extract cannabis and it's delicious.

The only thing you have to pay attention to is to procure some good old unprocessed fat milk. It should be boiled along with the weed at the lowest temperature for as long as it takes. You can also use leaves and even the stem or the males – it would be less potent but still remarkably psychoactive.

Stir from time to time and pay attention not to overcook it. It's ready when the milk has condensed to a very dense consistency, becoming viscous and yellow-green.

Of course, you can use it as it is or add it to cakes or whatever else you find appropriate.

Cookies

If you haven't experienced cookies so far, you're not a real pot-head. And I'm saying "experienced" because eating would just be inadequate. The cookies are so tasty that they will make you forget that they're actually concentrated weed-bombs and you will end up realizing this when it's too late, when the whole tray is finished. Now, that is a real over dose experience that most of us had, by mistake, but such a sweet mistake after all.

So, here's how to make some simple magic cookies. But first of all, you have to decarb your weed because the cooking time and temperature won't be enough for that.

Ingredients: 300g butter, 20g sugar, one pinch of salt, 2 eggs, 500g flour and about 20g weed. Pre-heat the oven at 105° C. And in the meantime, mix the ingredients – first the butter and sugar, gradually adding the eggs, salt and the grinded decarbed weed. Slowly add the flour too; kneading till the dough is consistent and elastic enough to bake. Put the dough in some biscuit forms or just design your own and spread them in the tray that you have previously thinly greased with butter. Place the tray in the oven and let them bake. The cookies are ready when their edges have turned slightly brown.

Enjoy, but be mindful, this tray is to be shared.

More than an industry, the use of the cannabis plant is a culture. One that lives and perpetuates through its passionate consumers, who entrust it with love and respect. It can only be so.

Therefore, it is crucial that we never stop experimenting, that we enroll our energy and imagination into growing and processing, that we never stop learning. Because there will always be better methods of extraction, less intrusive and there still are so many new things to learn about cannabis properties. Although we have come millennia holding hands with the marijuana plant, we are just at the beginning of our study in terms of scientific knowledge. There still is so much more to research and discover about cannabinoids and terrenes.

So, learn, try, enjoy and share.

Peace and love.

www.ingramcontent.com/pod-product-compliance
Lightning Source LLC
Chambersburg PA
CBHW071323280526
45788CB00004B/1995